STUDY

≋ OF THE ≋

RAFT

The Colorado Prize for Poetry

STUDY

≈≈ OF THE ≈≈

RAFT

POEMS

Leonora Simonovis

The Center for Literary Publishing
Colorado State University

For information about permission to reproduce
selections from this book, write to
The Center for Literary Publishing
attn: Permissions
9105 Campus Delivery
Colorado State University
Fort Collins, Colorado 80523-9105.

Printed in the United States of America.

"Night Duty" by Tomas Tranströmer, translated by Robin Fulton, from
The Great Enigma, copyright © 1987, 1997, 2002, 2006 by Tomas Tranströmer.
Translation © 1987, 1997, 2002, 2006 by Robin Fulton.
Reprinted by permission of New Directions Publishing Corp.

Adalber Salas Hernández, excerpt from "Las cosas, como las palabras,"
from *Río en Blanco* (Sudaquia Editores, 2016) page 63.
Used by permission of the author.

Library of Congress Cataloging-in-Publication Data

Names: Simonovis, Leonora, author.
Title: Study of the raft : poems / Leonora Simonovis.
Description: Fort Collins : The Center for Literary Publishing, [2021]
Identifiers: LCCN 2021033206 (print) | LCCN 2021033207 (ebook) | ISBN
9781885635792 (paperback) | ISBN 9781885635808 (ebook)
Subjects: LCGFT: Poetry.
Classification: LCC PS3619.I562865 S78 2021 (print) | LCC PS3619.I562865
(ebook) | DDC 811/.6--dc23
LC record available at https://lccn.loc.gov/2021033206
LC ebook record available at https://lccn.loc.gov/2021033207

The paper used in this book meets the minimum requirements of the
American National Standard for Information Sciences-Permanence of Paper
for Printed Library Materials, ANSI Z39.48-1984.

Para mi mamá, por todo

Las cosas, como las palabras, recuerdan lo que no han vivido.
—Adalber Salas Hernández

The language marches in step with the executioners.
Therefore, we must get a new language.
—Tomas Tranströmer

CONTENTS

UNO

Maps

In the beginning we
        were yellowbrownblueblack
                stalks   teeth clattering
for wind ground
             with mortar
and pestle   scattered
                    into ocean.
No snake in this
        story   no body to tempt
and exile   on the seventh
      day the rivers
             bruised like drumskin.

We are children
             of corn and fish bones
cleaved by starlight
        and spit   thousands
of years tall
            and still untamed
our homes taken we
      dream the pestle
as mortar.

Our mothers' hips
      carry the embers
of dawn
           their hands yield
the sweetest dough

cradle our faces
brush crumbs
off our lips
we eat so we remember
how bodies
are sharpened   wrought.

We rinse stories
out of the sea
that was river.
They shape-shift
into kernels   rewrite
themselves in orbit
For a moment   words
hover at the edge
of consciousness
For a moment we
are a sketch
of our own
making.

Water Rituals

Abuela's body a husk
        like the corn we wash,
dehair and cook for hours.

River water, she says,
        for the baptism.
Her child dead at seven

from malaria. Abuela,
        a nurse, couldn't
save him. *River water,*

she says again and again.
        She wants to wear
her navy blue polyester

dress *for the baptism.*
        When we were
children we baptized

our dolls with holy
        water. Now all we
have is a ghost-child

and we play, dress Abuela
        up, rub camphor oil
on her skin, her arms and face

polished slick as a river stone.

Of Mouths and Tongues

She lets the tongue
—la lengua—out on a leash

then reels her back, an act
of love and a habit. Lengua

both muscle—memory—and language—
Mother Tongue—a voice at the back

of the mouth. I want to write a book
called the lengua of my boca

since speaking my lengua is
becoming a forgotten art.

In the news they talk
about a man found this side

of the river—boca de río—
he spoke another lengua,

was on his back, open-
mouthed, tongue unabridged.

Father-Lengua

My father speaks English
with "peros" and "itos."
His pointer fingers cross
   one
   on top
   of the other
to push away mal de ojo.
His right hand quickly
makes the sign of the cross.
He's a master in lip-pointing,
mouth puckering towards an object
or person, no need for translation.
I tell him he's a polyglot;
his body speaks where words fail.
People comment on his accent,
mispronounce his name,
call him *Ex-savior,*
as if he had fallen
from grace and could
not be redeemed.
Shah vee air he says
     —over and over—
It's Basque. But they think
Basque is a painter.
When I buy him
coffee, I take the cup from
the barista's hand and write
his name as many times
as it takes for all to see.

Still Life with Baby

Baby José	inside Abuela's
pink and white	armoire
floating	in a jar of alcohol
Ten perfect fingers	bony knees bent

—as if in prayer—

Seven months	for a body
to unclench	to unload genealogy
from the navel	down a staircase
Abuelo driving	a roiling storm
the doctor's	calculated words
his peace offering	*you can keep the body*
Abuela's guilt	locked in a jar
a pasty doll	the size of a mother's breath.

Arabian Nights (Remix)

Caracas, February 4, 1992

Tonight, a commander in olive
uniform declares war against
the background of a TV studio
*—Now and forever, this revolution
will be recorded in the annals of history.*
My mother's foot softly taps
on the floor and for a moment
the camera wobbles, but the commander
doesn't seem to notice. I clutch
my copy of *Arabian Nights,*
the cover scabbed and peeling,
trace the outlines of domed
palaces and flying carpets half-
heartedly colored by the book's
previous owners. *Everyone
believes a silver-tongue,* says one
character after listening to Scheherazade
lull the sultan to sleep. The commander
calls everyone to arms—*Justice will
come swiftly to those who oppose us.*
I consider my parents' warnings
*—if we don't come home, someone
will keep you safe*—their faces
flickering in and out of view
in the bluish light of the screen
while between the pages,
a woman gets to live another day.

Katsaridaphobia

It wasn't so much the smell
of rancid oil but how they

starred the ceiling, many-legged
nightmares falling on our beds.

If I paid attention, I could see
their constellations shifting.

I called them Azabache, Canela,
Luna, Lucero, like the horses we

rode at the farm. Tame. Familiar.
Mamá scolded me for not killing

them, but the sound of death
is not meant for every ear.

How many times did I panic
when wings smacked my body,

when legs skittered on an arm
or leg? The only time I stepped

on a roach, the scene repeated
in my head like a horror film.

I kept looking at the corpse,
unnerved by postmortem spasms.

It's easier to run, brush the fear
away. But maybe I should
have asked them, *What is my name?*

The Holy Family

I

The Sister talks
of *our ever present*
and loving Father.
I said He let His son die,
asked if resurrection
is the power to fly
and had to write,
I must not question
my Lord 100 times.
I read about Lucifer's
fall. *It will happen*
to you, the Sister
says. When my family
was exiled a car took us
to the airport.

Outside, we heard the mountain race past.
Inside, our bodies muzzled by fear.

Lucifer didn't fall. He was pushed
for being different, and what broke
were not his wings but his will.
You'll know he's here when
you smell sulfur. But isn't
sulfur a yellow-winged butterfly?

2

The Sister says He'll come
for me because I wished
my father dead. *Pecado,*
she says, *honor your mother
and father.* She tells me
how many of the Ten
Commandments I've
broken. I've never been
good with numbers. I sit
on my bed, shaking.
He's home.
One hand on his belt.

3

The devil in the Sister's forked
tongue. I've seen her sweat and lick
her lips before His naked torso.
All the sisters eat His body, drink
from Him. The Bible says don't kill
or lust after another's property.
My uncle's mistress went to court.
So greedy, people said, *a husband
and a lover? Una puta.*
She lost everything.

It's Not an Act

He must have never played the
            piano or he'd know
how to read silence.

I can't remember his
            name, and he never
asked for mine. Black slacks,

a striped collared shirt,
            a boy dressed as man,
fingers pressed into my back.

I think of piglets outside
            Abuelo's town, running
towards a shack where a woman

watches from the threshold,
            the stink of manure
and dried blood crusting

her grimace. The boy's legs
            scissored with mine,
dull edged, static. I want to leave.

But I don't. The space between
            running and choosing

to leave is the scream
            that breaks my throat open.

I've Been Prey for Most of My Life

In the subway a man pressed
      against
my hips. On the bus a hand
      on my
thigh. Someone's sweat drips
      onto
my pores. Eyes lift up my skirts, crawl
      inside
my shirt. At home my mother's uncle
tangos his legs between mine
      —*Let me*
show you, get closer. My hand
in his. His other hand
      I don't remember.

My mother howls, pounds her fists on his
chest, pulls our shadows apart. She knows
what it is to be hunted, to dodge the bullets
of others' desire. We shroud ourselves
in silence, and still they come, call us names.
Virgen   puta   madre   puta   hija
don't let them touch you don't give
yourself away don't don't don't don't

Gospel

After Onechot's "Rotten Town"

Bullet drops spit
on the bus's plastic
windows. Clothes

They live in a Rotten city

glued to skin, bodies
steam in the aisle. Green
uniforms & red

They live in a Rotten city

berets on every corner.
In this city we walk
with those already gone,

They live in a Rotten city

transformed in the red
cocoon of a failed revolution.
The river's overflow

They live in a Rotten city

drags pieces of tin roofs, a
door, a diaper, food
wrappers. "Two Hundred

They live in a Rotten city

Murders This Week" reads
a headline. We march to
honor the fallen: students,

They live in a Rotten city

mothers, fathers, brothers,
sisters, sons and daughters,
bodies piling at the morgue,

They live in a Rotten city

untagged, unclaimed,
unbagged and bound
to a trigger. Murder

They live in a Rotten city

as prayer and redemption.
*Why can't I have what they
have?* says a prisoner

They live in a Rotten city

when asked about his
criminal activities.
At the bus station,

They live in a Rotten city

street vendors sell 30-cm
statues of former criminals
—heroes?—so when a child

They live in a Rotten city

takes a life, they know
they'll always be forgiven.

Revolutionary

Caracas, Venezuela, March 2019

Luisa's boy pulls a McDonald's
wrapper from the trash and licks
the ketchup off it. At the morgue,

soldiers thrift bullets from already
cold flesh. *Have you ever held
a gun? Felt its sorrow-heavy body?*

A red beret is not a trend but a uniform,
which is man and gun or maybe a song
with the word *freedom,* a spell for eager crowds.

But the problem has never been the boy's
hunger, the lack of bullets, the clothes.

It's the song. Listen to it. Tell me
when the voice you hear is your own.

Mozart in the XXI Century

He plays the national anthem
on his violin while people cradle
a yellow, blue, and red flag. Seven
white stars drop from the fringe.

      They sing, *Gloria al bravo pueblo,* arms
      in the air, mouths shaped like the tip
      of a gun. The "o" in *pueblo* barrels
      with such force, ten police officers
      surround the boy—what was he: 18, 19?—
      and yank away his violin. *That bow's*
      a weapon, says one. *Sing with us,*
      the boy says, *ustedes son pueblo también.*
      Their loyalty is out of tune with their uniforms.

The boy in a cell.
His fingers broken.
Outside the crowd swells
like his bruised jaw,
their song unstoppable.

Once he heard them
through the ringing in his ears.
Once they surrounded his city,
a memory in black and white.
Once he strung a melody
on the echoes of thunder.

Circus

A man once held a gun
to my stomach, his eyes

looking beyond. As a kid,
I watched a trainer prod

an elephant's body into submission
with an electric rod. Another

put his head inside a lion's
maw, the creature's eyes

as unnerved as the man
who held his gun tight

against my stomach,
trembling like the elephant's

feet while balanced on a tiny
block, like the lion as he smelled

fresh prey he couldn't touch.
In my dreams I see not the glassy

look of animals but an eye,
a finger, a trigger.

A body can only hold
so much before

it lets it all go.

Postcards from Everywhere and Nowhere

Dear Cousin,

I just landed.
At the airport, a picture
of a ship

crowning a wave.
A figure
on the prow waits,

like you on the tarmac
looking somewhere
ahead.

I waved and you did
not wave back.

Maybe you couldn't
see me.

Dear Cousin,

I chant, *I'm home,*
every day.

How many times
will it take
to feel it?

The monarchs
are starting
to cocoon.

Do you know
if, when they
transform,

they forget their past?

Dear Cousin,

Papers are important
in this land.

My neighbor told
me about Chinese
paper sons who invented
new identities
so they could stay.

I think of the paper
dolls we played with,
how we unfolded
each tab of the wedding
dress and turned
it into confetti.

Dear Cousin,

What happens when
your genetic
code is grafted

in two languages?
Does it mean
the patterns
never stop
shifting?

Yesterday we had
an earthquake
in San Diego

and I heard
the earth grinding
its teeth,

as if to speak.

Dear Cousin,

My son asked
if *citizen* is
a foreign
word.

I was tempted to say yes.

I told him
there was
once a city
whose people
were not alien.

They belonged.

*Oh, so where do we
belong?* he asked.

DOS

Diaspora Suite

There's an invisible línea where
a mouth clamps every syllable
shut: *Speak english. Get papeles.*
Reel in your rr's. Stow
all secrets under your tongue,
hide them from the ones invading
your mouth. Stand at the threshold.
Show them crossing
is not transgressing. If you
waylay light it becomes a part
of you, dissecting body into face/arms/
hands/feet and other unnameable objects.

*

After the flight I stumble down
a metal staircase, shudder in the sun's
insipid warmth. To my right the Pacific
glints like an odorless element. A customs
officer asks question after question
after question. I autocorrect and apologize,
going over prepositions and past tense
conjugations, think about TV shows
where Colgate smiles invite viewers to bleach
themselves into perfection. This is
no Hollywood movie, and I am not arriving.
My name an unpronounceable obstacle.

*

A cab driver asks where I'm from. I say
farther than Mexico, no English. I say we
fry the fish whole and suck on the eye
for luck until all that remains is a little
white ball rolling erres on the tongue. I say
we watch lightning pry open the horizon.
Sounds like a wonderful place.
You have beautiful skin.
Your teeth are very white.
My abuela told me about a little boy
who opened his mouth to show his teeth.
No scars on his back, so a planter
bought him. He had beautiful skin too.
I finger my passport, its corners
lifting like the hook on a fish's
lip pulling up memories.

*

The officer sorts bones in an orderly fashion,
        femurs and scapulas and a humerus
        disconnected from its radius.
        One sternum polka dotted by bullet holes.
He tags the bones with green pieces
of paper that don't translate into cards,
a living wage, a hospital bed.

He flexes his muscles, ripped from chasing
the ghosts who left behind this mess.
He couldn't catch them grab them
grind them so there would be no evidence
like there is now. Sand, dirt, and marrow:
dust of my dust, says the Bible.

*

A goat's carcass dozes on hot coals,
flavors infused by soil and dung.
Men tear meat pinked by the setting sun.
They drink aguardiente, slice grains
of sand with their blades, toss them
in the water to exorcise their fears.
Living on the border they grow
stories from seed, toss them
over the fence, loosing La Llorona and
Huitzilopochtli on the other side.
*If you swallow a fallen star you can
cross on the back of a flying coyote,*
they tell the children, *like Aladdin and
the genie.* They never tell them
el Norte means nowhere.

*

Ysabel looks at the other
bodies. *No puedo aguantar
más.* Her Spanish both *refuge*
and obstacle. She left
her home and *two children*
in *Venezuela* after being *kidnapped,
robbed, shot,* marked as enemy
by her government.

*Panama City, Bogotá, Cancún
Mexico City, and Mexicali.*

North is freedom. Or was.
When her children wore
Carnaval costumes in Caracas,
they believed they were
Wonder Woman and Batman,
ready to fight crime.
She wants to believe but her faith
has already expired. She slips
her fingers through the bars
to touch another caged human.

TRES

Legends

Waraira Repano is the indigenous name of the mountain that surrounds the valley of Caracas.

1857	renamed Ávila, the mountain embraces the city growing on its hem, nursing it to life.
Caracas	whoever summits the highest peak claims it.
Boundaries	stones scattered over the early treads of tapirs.
Gazing	through a piece of X-ray film, we remember the story of a conquistador to be sacrificed.
History	he predicted a solar eclipse. The Mayas offered his heart to the sun. This is not taught in school.
School	abuelas counting beads on a rosary, praying their nietos remember a shell is also a body.
Remember	to serve coffee in tiny plastic cups—con leche, marrón, guayoyo, negrito, guarapo.

Tongue

one sip scorching the tip,
that space where words
are forgotten and recovered.

Words

salvaged, domesticated, skewed,
unraveled, the aftertaste
of something familiar.

Familiar

a skyline, a mountain, a city
resting against green. Up close
the sounds of ripping seams.

Seams

every decade foundations waver,
a tooth falls and speech lisps, the
tongue shifts into bone.

Bone

underneath layers of sediment,
jaguar, snake, mother of pearl,
the forgotten name of the ocean.

Further Study of the Raft

Hope can't hold
the logs together.

There's nowhere
beyond these Caribbean

waters. A voyage
built on a lie.

People move
from one collapsed

world to another,
visions of food

on phones and TV screens.
But on this raft

the food's gone
and sunburnt bodies sink,

throats scoured
by salt and fish scales.

At the Airport

The young woman
stands like an unmoored

sentence, red-rimmed
eyes roaming the crowds.

Next to her a young man—her
boyfriend?—and her mother.

He lifts his hand, as if wanting
to touch the parts of her he wants

to remember, but the woman
has already turned the page.

Sometimes the only way out is
to step into the fable of another

existence. Every few minutes
a flash of military green, raised voices,

another passenger detained
and hassled for a few dollars.

Things to remember:
you are a one-way ticket.
Say goodbye, not hasta luego.

To leave is to tune in to your
own unraveling, to understand
that forever is also never.

The woman holds her loved ones,
stands up, wobbles, straightens.

*Call us when you get
to the gate,* the mother says.

Venezuelan Mosaic

1

The line running out the makeshift
market a mile long, each person's
hunger a number on sunburnt skin.

2

Inside the market two women
roll on the ground, pull at each
other's hair for an extra carton of milk.

3

On Morrocoy Beach a monster
truck backs into the water. Under
the truck's wheels, broken turtle eggs.

4

A mob surrounds a meat truck, beats
its sides like a piñata. Someone yells
para todos. The barrio will eat today.

5

Naked bodies on the concrete floor.
The morgue workers swing and toss.
No black bags, no electricity, no tags.

6

A worker lifts a wilted boy from
a pyramid of flesh, seven black holes
in his chest. The father touches each one,

7

spits out his pain. A mother comes
to identify her oldest son and finds
her youngest among the ruins.

8

What is police brutality? asks a five-
year-old. In the news a young man's
ghost outlined in chalk. The father turns

9

the TV off. A revolution is not
televised but broadcast in hues
of red—a T-shirt, a beret, a heart,

10

stuttering mid-sentence, scattering
pomegranate seeds into the earth.
It looks like blood, somebody says.

11

It's not, an officer responds,
holstering his conscience.
The evidence is in the pit.

Still Life in Exile

Papá calls again:
your cousin died in jail
a policeman came last night
says I'm on the list.

A grocery list on my night table.

I left a country where politicians
play in red berets while people
die for a pair of shoes.

Hunger has too many faces.

Papá's short-circuited breath brings
me back: *people are disappearing.* You can't
make this up, yet people write books about it.

The silence of citizenship.

My lips press against the screen;
on the other end, the fear of betrayal.

Coup de Folie 1

After Leonora Carrington

White coats
    skulk
        behind
me
        I long
    to ride
Pegasus
    but he cannot
        cross
the threshold
    of Cardiazol
        unlike
the Gorgon
        I
    cannot
turn
        contempt
into bread
        and stone
    The coats
form
        a triangle
take me
        with them
    I want
a version
        of myself
that will

break
        the cords
   binding
my mane
       and tail
to a bed
   where
Perseus
   places
       a mirror
in front
   of me
   then breaks it
       He doesn't
understand
   I worship
       myself
because I see
       myself
   complete

Coup de Folie 2

The day Aunt C. went
        missing, she'd been

pulling out her hairs
        by the roots.

Her neighbors found
        a pill bottle full.

She used them
        to ensnare the voices

and confuse them.
        When I found

her, she was living
        under a bridge, a Janus-

headed goddess wearing
        a mantle and clawing

portals in the air. *A refuge,*
        she said, palpating

the wind. It took three nurses
        to put her in the sanatorio

van. The doctors said the tear
        could never be mended.

When I visited, Aunt C. clapped
        flamenco beats until the horizon

gobbled the face of the sun.
        On her night table brown hairs
tangled among white, grubby pills.

Arches

My mouth opens for the drill.
       I clench my fists to block a
childhood memory—same office,

different doctor, more pain.
       It helps to think of the dentist
as an architect repairing

structural cracks so the maxilla
       won't topple onto the mandible
and speech can remain able-bodied.

An arch holds the weight of whatever
       is above it. My mouth
embraces every two-tongued word

that translates self for others. If my teeth
       fall, my world collapses.
The doctor tells me I am deceiving

myself, but there's no substitute
       for bone. In the waiting room,
an older woman who's lost all

of her teeth says she had to learn
       to modulate by peeling back
the skin of syllables. Her tongue

slithers between worn pillars,
       licking each word into perfection.

Bellum Civile

The Reina Sofia a Dalí landscape.
        Within these walls time's
preserved in oil and linen.

Bodies spread against the walls,
        draping over benches, seeking
relief from this Madrid summer.

 A woman sketches *The Smile of*
        the Flamboyant Wings, hand
fluttering trance-like up and down

the page. We cross half-lit thresholds
        to finally arrive at the alcove
where Picasso's *Guernica* hangs

among the quiet devotion of visitors.
        In the silence my mother's words,
A civil war is kin against kin.

My brother and I fight a lot,
        but I know she means what we
witness on the black-and-white screen

of our TV: a name   a body   a gun.
        It's impossible to look and not label:
bull-mother   pigeon-child   dead-burning

house-light   bulb-woman   raised-man
  arms-pleading   the eye
of the bomb—the eye is the bomb. Horror

just a stanchion away. A sign screams
        FAVOR NO TOCAR/PLEASE DO
NOT TOUCH. What is there to touch?

Still Life with Smoked Landscape

California burns stories into ashes:
a man picks up a rabbit from the side

of a road, a couple watch
the flames from inside

their swimming pool,
hands together in prayer.

After their rescue no one
asked if the water was hot

or what it felt to be island.
People's eyes lock on phone

screens while outside rages
orange. My kitchen table

scratched—one vertical line
for each life lost. In Julio

Cortázar's "House Taken
Over," the owners are chased

away by voices. Fire can
speak but we'd rather not hear.

From my window, I see monarchs
fall, wings singed in mid-flight.

Prayers unanswered.

Bedtime Stories

Every witch moth has
      a pact with death.

All night she soars towards
      light, until paralyzed

by pleasure, she plummets,
      bending gravity around

the center of her own galaxy.
      In the stories, bat-shaped

wings the color of the devil's
      dreams deprive children

of sight. In the morning, a mother
      finds the witch moth's body

splayed as if waiting to be read.
      There's something satisfying

about open endings, like the story
      I made up where you and I

find an eagle's feather and graze
      its barb, fingers flushed

with the promise of flight.

Questions

For my mother

What does it feel
like to open the archive
of Abuela's heart and not

find the seven letters
that make your name?
I don't have a daughter,

she says to you when
you feed her. Will you ever
stop seeing me? Abuela

has a baby doll. *Mi bebé,*
she says. She dresses
and feeds her, sings

her a song you thought
she had forgotten,
the same one she hummed

when you couldn't sleep.
I believe Abuela hears
when you say you'll

never leave her, like I
did when my hand barely
fit into your own.

Apology in Blue

For my brother A.

Mamá said *I had*
      to love you,
      take care of you,
      look out for you.

I became a river current
      cutting through

rock, unbridled. When we
      tugged on a thread-

bare rope I yanked and let
      go, knowing you'd fall.

I wanted to hurt the blue of you
      I couldn't have, the one she

said wasn't meant for me, because
      girls don't dream in blue.

I didn't anticipate the cut on the back
      of your head, your screams,

Mamá's hands reeking of peroxide,
      the rusty trace of blood. She

didn't understand why our bodies
      repelled each other, why I

couldn't love you like she did.
      I longed to say it was not

about love, but that every patch
      of blue is an ocean.

What Happens When We Die?

my son asks as I put him to bed.
It's not so much the body

but the absence of hair
in the bathroom sink,

a rusty razor, a bag of clothes
left for the shelter to pick

up, the lingering scent
of rose water and aftershave.

We can forget a voice
and the texture of skin

but scent remains.
Will you miss me when I die?

I lay my head on his pillow,
place my hand on the hollow

his body makes when he
turns towards the wall.

The scent of fresh grass
clippings, vanilla, and sweat.

My right ear muffled, I tell
him about conversations

underwater. We know
the words don't matter,

only shaping our mouths
around the heaviness

of water. If I could draw
my fear of losing him,

it would look like an empty
toy room, light stealing

through closed curtains.
The scent of fresh grass

clippings, vanilla, sweat,
dust settling onto a hollow bed.

I Am Not Leaving

There's a brittle quality
to plant life, a browning

that disintegrates to the touch
and sticks to the skin. I am

not from this land but of it,
the body an unwanted guest.

I've learned to ignore the glare
of morning, to read the glyphs

of ashes, to groan with a coastal
oak. During the summer months

the hawks quiet and my aural
map feels incomplete, disjointed,

yet alert to the smallest glimpse
of a fir sprouting in lieu of life

or maybe because of it. A farmer
once told me about "prescribed

burns," and before he explained I
thought of a pharmacy prescription

no one would refill, which shows
how little I know about the subject.

I've come to understand that in this
land, fire consumes to make space

for new language, one I cannot
speak, so I touch the surfaces

around me, whisper incantations,
wave my arms above my head,

baptize myself with whiskey
until my skin begins to peel

like the crimson leaves
of a maple, and all that is left

is the crusty skin of old earth.
Under it, all the words at my disposal.

Notes

The epigraphs at the beginning of the book contain lines from Adalber Salas Hernández's poetry collection *Río en blanco* (2016) and from Tomas Tranströmer's "Night Duty," included in *The Great Enigma: New Collected Poems* (2006).

The date in "Arabian Nights (Remix)" represents the day on which the now-deceased former Venezuelan president Hugo Chávez enacted his first coup d'état attempt in Caracas and took over a government TV network to deliver his message.

"Gospel" uses a line from Venezuelan singer and composer Onechot's main hit, "Rotten Town," which was released in 2008. The song represents the terrible conditions in which people from lower socioeconomic status live in the city of Caracas, Venezuela. It especially focuses on gun violence.

"Mozart in the XXI Century" was inspired by Venezuelan musician and activitst Wuilly Arteaga, who was detained and tortured by authorities in 2017 for protesting against the Maduro regime while playing his violin in public.

"Revolutionary" was inspired by Venezuelan author Raquel Rivas Rojas's crime novels *Muerte en el Guaire* and *El accidente,* in which the narrators describe the deterioration of the city of Caracas and its people.

The last stanza in "Diaspora Suite" was inspired by a *New York Times* opinion article by Francisco Cantú titled "Seeking Refuge, Legally, and Finding Prison." It begins with the following description: "For more than seven months, Ysabel has been incarcerated without bond at an immigrant detention center in southern Arizona, part of a vast network of for-profit internment facilities administered by private companies under contract with the Department of Homeland Security." The italicized words in the poem are borrowed from the article.

The last four lines in "Coup de Folie 1" are from Leonora Carrington's *Down Below,* with a change in verb tense. The original reads, "I worshipped myself because I saw myself complete."

Acknowledgments

This book is the product of collective effort, and I'm thankful to the editors and readers of these publications in which previous versions of the following poems appeared:

"Of Mouths and Tongues," *Inverted Syntax.*
"Still Life with a Baby," *A Year in Ink, Vol. 10.*
"I've Been Prey for Most of My Life," *The Rumpus.*
"Mozart in the xxi Century," *Diode Poetry Journal.*
"Revolutionary" and "Circus," *The Arkansas International.*
"Further Study of the Raft," *Gargoyle Magazine.*
"Father-Lengua," *Tinderbox Poetry Journal.*
Part of "Diaspora Suite" was published in the *San Diego Poetry Annual* and *The Acentos Review.*

Two of the poems from "Postcards from Everywhere and Nowhere" were featured in the chapbook *I Traveled West: Poets on Place and Belonging* as part of an initiative from the Contemporary Irish Arts Center Los Angeles (CIACLA), which brought five international poets together to consider and reflect on themes of home, place, and migration, among others.

Thank you to the readers and the editor at Perugia Press, who chose a previous version of this manuscript as a semifinalist for the 2021 Perugia Poetry Prize.

My deepest gratitude and appreciation to Sherwin Bitsui for seeing the value and promise in this manuscript. Thank you to the Center for Literary Publishing (CLP) at Colorado State University (CSU) and the University Press of Colorado (UPC). Thank you, Stephanie G'Schwind and Beth Svinarich, for your care and attention during the publication process.

Thank you, Natalie, Daisy, and all the staff and faculty at the Antioch University Los Angeles MFA program. Huge thanks to my mentors, for inspiring me to be the best version of myself, both as a writer and as a person. To Victoria Chang, for seeing what I couldn't and for guiding me through the process of finding my own way; to Jim Daniels, for your generosity, enlightening conversations, and for helping me choose a title for the manuscript; to Blas Falconer, for your careful edits and for teaching me to listen and observe during revision; to Vandana Khanna, for showing me that every word, every line, and every poem has its own place, even if we can't see it yet; to Jaswinder Bolina, for challenging me in unexpected ways, and for our shared love of language; to Ari Banias, for your kind words and detailed observations; to Xochitl-Julisa Bermejo for your enthusiasm and for inspiring me to discover that where I am is where I need to be.

Thank you to the brilliant poets and writers at Antioch who read many of these poems and helped me bring them to life: Margaret Kean, Merry Dennehy, Sarah Hass, Jordan Nakamura, Julia Knowles, Jeri Frederickson, Alisha Escobedo, Cristina Medina, Maya Nordine, Ale Cruz, Jake Bailey, Amanda Lopez, Aliah Lavonne-Tigh, and Josh Ryan.

To Ruth Foreman, for embodying the physicality of writing. And to Willie Perdomo, for teaching the value of writing the hard poem. Gracias VONA family: Joy, Adelina, Pacyinz, Yamini, Angelina, Vanessa, Karla, Sergio, Gabriel, Ana and Irene. You inspire me.

Thank you to the Speakeasy staff, workshop peers and mentors Eloisa Amezcua and Luther Hughes. Love and gratitude to my dear Rosebud Ben-Oni, for showing me the importance of lifting each other up and for all of your generous suggestions and comments.

Thank you, Molly Bess, Peter Mason, Bailey Hutchinson, and the team at Open Mouth Literary Center; Franny Choi and Nate Marshall, donia, and all the beautiful folx at the Open Mouth Poetry Retreat. Thank you, David Brunson, for understanding my work and for bringing it to light.

Thank you, Death Rattle Writers Festival and *Inverted Syntax*, Ashley Howell and Nawal Nader-French, for the shout-outs and support.

Huge thanks to my editor and friend at *Drizzle Review*, Rebecca Valley, for your generosity of spirit and capacity to listen with an open heart.

Thank you, Jenny Minniti-Shippey and CIACLA, for giving my voice a space and a place to expand and to grow.

Thank you, Erin Redfern, for your thoughtful comments on the "Coup de Folie" poems and for helping me promote my work.

Thank you to Dean Noelle Norton, in the College of Arts and Science at the University of San Diego, and to my department chair, colleague, and friend, Rebecca Ingram, for your continued support. To my colleagues in the LCL department and the Spanish program at USD, thank you. To my students, thank you for being such amazing teachers.

Love and gratitude to my writing sister and friend, Yamini Pathak, for your kindness and encouragement. To dear Patrick Mullen-Coyoy, for your keen observations and suggestions. And to Margaret Kean and Merry Dennehy for sharing the joy of learning, curiosity, and friendship.

To my family, my abuela Rosa and bisabuela Berta for teaching me that connection to the land and to our ancestors can heal us and hold us. To my parents, Nelson and Leonora, for instilling in me the love of reading and for encouraging me to follow my heart. Mamá, wherever you are, this one is for you. To my siblings, Alejandro and Juan Pablo, for the laughs and for being my rocks when I most needed it (even if you didn't know it). And to my sisters (in-law), Ina and Yulie, whose strength I find inspiring. To my primos, primas, tíos, and tías. We are all over the world, but never apart. Thank you for showing me that distance only makes our love stronger.

To Chris, who believes in me more than I do. Thank you for holding the space for me and for the encouragement. And to our beautiful boys, Santiago and Mateo, who feel very proud to have "una mama poeta." I love you all.

This book is set in Corundum Text Book and Oswald
by The Center for Literary Publishing
at Colorado State University.

Copyediting by Annmarie Delfino.
Proofreading by Ross Reagan.
Book design and typesetting by Megan Lear.
Cover design by Stephanie G'Schwind.
Cover art by Fabio Santaniello Bruun.
Printing by Books International.